E L E M E N T A R Y

CONVERSATION

M arion Geddes
Gill Sturtridge

PRENTICE HALL

Published 1998 by Prentice Hall Europe
Campus 400, Spring Way
Maylands Avenue, Hemel Hempstead
Hertfordshire, HP2 7EZ

A division of Simon & Schuster International

First Published 1992 by Macmillan Publishers Limited

Illustrations by Helen Ganly
Produced by AMR

Printed and bound in Great Britain by The Bath Press, Bath

A catalogue record for this book is available from
the British Library

ISBN 0-13-404997-7

6   5   4

1999   98

Acknowledgements

The publisher would like to thank the following for permission to use their
copyright material:

BBC Stills Library: p.29 (TV gallery);
Barnaby's Picture Library: pp29/Rees (pilot), 53 (peke and cat);
Sally and Richard Greenhill Photo Library: pp.11, 19 (family at table), 29 (judges);
Steve Richards: p. 29 (object pictures), 54;
Select Photos: p. 29. Nickson (catwalk model);
Spectrum Colour Library: pp. 19 (family walking), 29 (lifeguard), 53 (muzzle)

CONTENTS

ABOUT THIS BOOK

This book will help students become more confident about taking part in conversations in English. They will learn and practise the language necessary for important conversation skills. They will also learn to speak more accurately and more fluently on everyday topics.

The book is divided into two parts.

Part 1: Conversation skills practises important skills or strategies, such as how to get a conversation started, how to keep it going, and how to close a conversation.

All units in Part 1 follow the same format:

Recognizing skills contextualises the conversation skill being practised in the unit. Dictation of key phrases focuses attention on the skill and on pronunciation. You may also wish to discuss with the students how the skill is realised in their own mother tongue and any differences there are with English.

The **Phrase box** in each unit gives key language for the skill.

Developing skills gives controlled practice in the skill and in some of the key language.

Using skills gives freer, more realistic practice in the skill.

Part 2: Conversation topics allows students to talk about the kinds of thing they are likely to talk about when striking up conversation in English in real life, either with native speakers or in situations where English is an international language. In other words, they can be themselves, participating in what is essentially a rehearsal for conversations outside the classroom.

Vocabulary boxes suggest useful words for the conversations. It is important for students to realise that a wide vocabulary is essential for conversational fluency. They should be encouraged to add their own words to the boxes.

Every unit in the book starts with a **warm up**. At the beginning of a lesson, this gives the students time to settle down and to get into an English-speaking frame of mind. If necessary, it also allows late-comers to slip into their seats before you get going on the main activities of the lesson. It is up to you to set an appropriate pace for these warm-ups, but generally you should make sure they are fairly fast and snappy.

In some warm-ups, stress and intonation are very important. In these cases, examples are given on the cassette. The text indicates how the cassette can be used.

Marion Geddes   *Gill Sturtridge*

PART ONE

Conversation Skills

STARTING A CONVERSATION

Warm up: Echoes

Your teacher will ask you some questions. You will answer by repeating the key word with falling intonation, like this:

T   We're going to play a game. OK?

S1 OK.

T   Are you ready?

S2 Ready.

Before you begin, you can use the cassette to practise intonation. You will hear two people asking and answering like this:

A OK?   **B** OK.

A Ready?   **B** Ready.

Listen. Then listen and repeat.

Recognizing skills

Task 1

You are going to listen to a conversation between two people who have just met each other. Close your book and listen.

Rewind the cassette. Listen again and read silently.

Anne	Gillian, I'd like you to meet Mustafa.
Gillian	Hello. My name's Gillian.
Mustafa	Hello. I'm sorry, what's your name?
Gillian	Gillian. G I double L I A N.
Mustafa	I'm Mustafa. Where are you from?
Gillian	I'm from England. And what about you?
Mustafa	I'm from Egypt.
Gillian	Oh? Where exactly do you live in Egypt?
Mustafa	Cairo. Have you been there?
Gillian	No, but I've heard it's an interesting place.
Mustafa	Yes it is. How long have you been here?
Gillian	Two weeks.
Mustafa	And are you here alone or with your family?

Gillian	I'm with my husband. What about you? Are you married?
Mustafa	No, I'm single. I'm here on business. And you?
Gillian	I'm on holiday. What do you do?
Mustafa	I'm an architect. I'm interested in old buildings.
Gillian	Oh, really? A friend of mine's an architect. Oh, hello David. Mustafa, this is David. David, this is Mustafa.
David	Pleased to meet you.

🔲 *Task 2*

You are going to hear eight phrases from the conversation. Listen and complete them.

1 .... meet Mustafa.

2 .... Gillian.

3 .... from?

4 What .... ?

5 .... alone or ....
family?

6 What .... ?

7 .... old buildings.

8 Pleased ....

In these phrases, many words are linked together.

a A consonant at the end of a word is often moved to the beginning of the next word. For example:

like you = li kyou   where are = whe rar

b Consonants become weak or disappear when two or three consonants come together. For example:

I'(d) like   ol(d) buildings

Rewind and listen to the phrases again. Find at least two more examples of (a) and (b).

🔲 *Task 3*

You will hear the whole conversation again, with pauses. Listen and repeat, trying to make links between words.

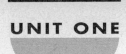
Phrase box

Introducing yourself	Hello. My name's ... I'm ...	Hello. I'm ... Hello, pleased to meet you.
Introducing someone else	This is ... I'd like you to meet ... *(more formal)* I'd like to introduce you to ...	Hello, nice to meet you. Oh, I've heard a lot about you (from X). How do you do.
Continuing the conversation by asking questions	Where are you from? Where exactly do you live in (Brazil)? What do you do? Have you got children? Are you married? Do you know (Cairo)? Do you know (Mary/Mary's brother)? Is this your first visit to ... ? Have you been here before? How long have you been here?	I'm from (Brazil). I'm a (student). I work for/in (a bank). I'm (single/divorced/separated).
Continuing the conversation by giving information	I'm here on (business/holiday). What about you? I'm interested in (music/playing the piano). And you?	

Developing skills

Task 1

Work in pairs. Read this conversation by matching the phrases. The first four have been marked for you.

A

(1)– Hello. My name's Francis.

– About a week. And you?

(3)– Where are you from?

– I like running – marathon running.

– No, but I've heard it's a lovely place.

– Where exactly in Canada?

– I'm here on business too. I'm an engineer. What do you do?

– No, I'm here alone. And you?

– What are you interested in?

B

(4)– I'm from Canada.

(2)– Hello, Francis. Nice to meet you. I'm Jo.

– About three weeks. I'm here on business.

– I work for a bank. Are you with your family?

– I'm alone too. I'm single.

– I play golf and I like swimming. What about you.?

– Montreal. Have you been there?

– Yes, it is. How long have you been here?

– I prefer walking!

Task 2

Work in pairs. Imagine you are meeting your partner for the first time. Start a conversation with your partner.

Using skills

Task 1

You are going to a party. Imagine a new character for yourself. Complete these notes.

Your name:

Your age:

Are you married/single?

Where do you live?

What do you do?

What are you interested in?

Now you are at the party. You don't know anyone. Walk around the room and meet some of the other guests. When you have talked to two or three of the guests, introduce them to each other.

Task 2

Work in pairs. Look at the photo opposite. **A**'s friend is in the photo. **B** wants to know more about him/her.

A: Choose one of the people in the photo. It is your friend. Before you tell **B** about him/her think about:
  • his/her name and age
  • where and when you met him/her
  • where he/she is from and where he/she lives
  • his/her job
  • his/her interests   etc.

B: Find out all you can about **A**'s friend by asking questions like these:
  • What's his/her name?
  • Where did you meet him/her?
  • Where is he/she from?

Think of at least ten questions.

When you are both ready, **B** will start the conversation by asking **A**: *Which one is your friend?*

unit 2

MAKING SURE YOU UNDERSTAND

Warm up: What did you say?

Your teacher will tell you about something. Pretend you don't understand the end of each sentence and ask questions. For example:

T I went on holiday last year with *my sister*.

S1 *Who* did you say?

T My sister. We went together to *New York*.

S2 *Where* did you say?

T New York. We went there in *August*.

S3 *When* did you say?

T In August.

Before you begin, you can use the cassette to listen to the example, and repeat these questions:

Who did you say?
Where did you say?
When did you say?
What did you say?
What kind did you say?
Which did you say?
Which museum did you say?
How often did you say?
How many did you say?
How much did you say?
How long did you say?

Recognizing skills

Task 1

A foreigner is a little lost and stops someone in the street. Close your book and listen to the conversation.

Rewind the cassette. Listen again and read silently.

Foreigner Excuse me, could you tell me where Grimsby Street is please?

Man Sorry, I didn't quite catch that.

Foreigner Grimsby Street. I'm trying to find Grimsby Street.

Man	How do you spell that?
Foreigner	G R I M S B Y.
Man	Oh yes. Grimsby Street. Right, it's not far. Go along this street, and you'll come to some traffic lights. Turn right ...
Foreigner	I'm sorry, could you speak more slowly please?
Man	I'll start again. Go along this street...
Foreigner	Yes.
Man	And you'll see some traffic lights.
Foreigner	I'm sorry, I don't understand. What is 'traffic'?
Man	Traffic lights? Er, red, orange, green. To stop the traffic.
Foreigner	Sorry, could you explain what 'traffic' is?
Man	Traffic? Cars, buses ...
Foreigner	Ah, yes, yes.
Man	So, at the traffic lights, turn right and then take the second on your left. That's Stag Street. Walk along Stag Street and Grimsby Street is the first on your left.
Foreigner	Er, sorry, could you repeat that please?
Man	At the traffic lights, turn right. OK?
Foreigner	OK.
Man	Then take the second on your left, Stag Street. Got it?
Foreigner	Got it.
Man	Go along Stag Street, and you'll see Grimsby Street on the left.
Foreigner	Thank you very much.
Man	Not at all.

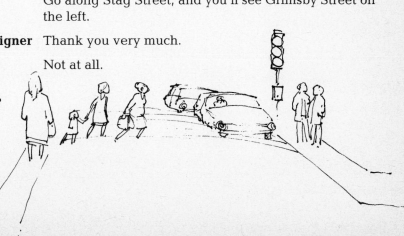

Task 2

You are going to hear six phrases from the conversation. Listen and complete them.

1   Sorry, I didn't ....

2   How .... that?

3   I'm sorry. .... more slowly .... ?

4   I'm sorry, I .... 'traffic'?

5   .... what 'traffic' is?

6   Sorry, ... that please?

Task 3

You will hear the phrases again, this time with pauses. Listen and repeat, remembering to make links between words.

Phrase box

Asking someone to repeat, speak more slowly, etc.	(I'm) sorry, Excuse me,	could you	repeat that please? speak more slowly?
			I didn't (quite) catch that.
			I don't understand.
	Sorry? Pardon?		

Asking about meaning, translation, spelling, pronunciation	What does X mean? What do you mean by X?		Sorry,	I don't know. I'm not sure.
	Could you	explain tell me	what an X is?	
	What is it What's it called What do you call it		in (Spanish)?	
	How do Can	you spell	X? this word?	
	How do you	say pronounce	this word? Y (in English)?	

PART ONE

UNIT TWO

Developing skills

Task 1

Work in pairs. This is a conversation in a library. Read it by matching the phrases. The first two are marked for you.

A	B
①– Good morning, can I help you?	– Could you repeat that please?
– Yes. DRI 463.014.	– D R I double F I E L D. Richard Driffield.
– How do you spell 'Driffield'?	– I'm not sure. But it's about (*cough*) cowboys and Indians.
– Ah, I know it. It's called *Cowboys in the Wild West.* Look under DRI 463.014.	– Thank you very much.
– Sorry, I didn't quite catch that.	②– Yes, I'm looking for a book by Richard Driffield.
– And what's the name of the book?	– Cowboys and Indians.

Task 2

Your teacher will tell you a story. Stop your teacher politely when you hear a word you don't know. For example:

T I'm going to tell you a story about an elf.

S1 Sorry, could you explain what an elf is?

Using skills

Work in pairs. You each have a letter from a friend. Prepare to read your letter aloud to your partner. Ask your teacher how to pronounce any word you are not sure about.

When you are ready, take turns to read your letter aloud. When you listen to your partner reading, interrupt continually to make sure you understand. Use phrases from the **Phrase Box**.
A's letter is on page 53.
B's letter is on page 54.

unit 3

MEETING SOMEONE YOU KNOW

Warm up: Talking about the weather

🔲 Listen to these phrases on the cassette. Then listen and repeat.

(It's a) lovely day, isn't it.	What miserable weather!
(Yes, isn't it) lovely.	(Absolutely) miserable.
beautiful.	awful.
gorgeous.	terrible.
great.	dreadful.
wonderful.	ghastly.
fantastic.	
marvellous.	Well, not as bad as yesterday!

Not bad. Better than yesterday.

Practise the phrases with your teacher. Then walk around the class talking about the weather with your friends. Try to use a different expression each time you speak to someone.

At first the weather is good. When your teacher claps hands, the weather suddenly changes to bad!

Recognizing skills

🔲 *Task 1*

You are going to hear a lot of people greeting each other at a party. Close your book and listen.

Rewind the cassette. Listen again and read silently.

Gillian Hello John. How are you?

John Not too bad. How are you?

Gillian Fine.

John And how's your mother?

Gillian She's very well thanks. Oh look, there's David. David, hi! How are things?

David Fine thanks. Oh, hello John. Haven't seen you for ages! Are you very busy at work?

John Quite busy. Oh, hello Anne. How are you? Everything OK?

Anne	Pretty good, thanks. And you? Still enjoying the job?
John	Yes. Working hard though. And you? Busy?
Anne	Quite busy. Oh, there's Gillian. I must say hello. Speak to you later, John. Hello Gillian. How are things?
Gillian	Not bad. David, do you know Anne?
David	Yes. Haven't seen you for ages, Anne. Have you been sick?
Anne	Well, I had flu last week.
David	Sorry to hear that. Are you OK now?
Anne	Yes, fine thanks.

Task 2

You are going to hear eight phrases from the conversation. Listen and complete them.

1   Hello John. .... you?

2   Not too bad. .... you?

3   .... thanks.

4   .... mother?

5   .... things?

6   .... for ages.

7   .... sick?

8   I'm sorry ....

Task 3

You will hear the conversation again, with pauses. Listen and repeat, remembering to make links between words.

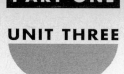

Phrase box

Initial greetings	How are you?	Fine thanks. And you?
	How are things?	Great.
	How are you doing?	Pretty good.
	Everything OK?	OK.
	How's life?	Alright.
	How's it going?	Not bad. Not too bad.
		So so.
Follow-up questions	How's your mother?	She's very well, thanks.
	Please give her my best wishes.	
	I haven't seen you for ages.	
	Have you been away?	
	sick?	
	ill?	
	off work?	
	Everything OK?	
	(Are you very) busy?	Quite busy.
		Pretty
	(Are you still) enjoying your job?	
	English course?	
	holiday?	
Moving to someone else	There's (David). I must say hello. I'll speak to you later (Gillian).	
Explaining past illness	I had (a touch of) flu.	
	I had a cold.	
	a sore throat.	
	a bad cough.	
	a bad back.	
	a stomach upset.	
Expressing sympathy	I'm sorry to hear that. Are you OK now?	
	alright	
Making sure two people know each other	You've met A.	
	Do you know A? Yes, we've known each other for ages.	

Developing skills

Task 1

Work in pairs. Match the phrases and read the conversation.

A	B
①– Hi Mary, how are you?	– Fine thanks. And how are you?
– It's fine. How's your brother?	– OK. I'll speak to you later.
– Not too bad.	– I haven't seen you for ages. Are you very busy?
– Quite busy.	– Are you still enjoying the job?
– There's Alan. I must say hello.	– Well, he had flu last week.
– I'm sorry to hear that. Is he OK now?	– Yes, pretty good.

Task 2

Work in pairs. Imagine these are English-speaking families that you both know well. Together decide their names.

The Greens

The Whites

A has news of the Green family. **B** has news of the White family. Look at the greetings in the **Phrase Box**. **A** asks **B** about each member of the White family. Then **B** asks **A** about the members of the Green family. For example:

A	How's Jimmie?	**B**	He's fine.
A	And Rachel? How is she?	**B**	She's not too bad. etc.

19

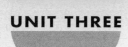
Using skills

You are going to go to a party.
If your birthday is on an odd date (1st, 3rd, 5th, 7th, 9th, etc.) you are
an old person, aged about 90.
If your birthday is on an even date (2nd, 4th, 6th, 8th, 10th, etc.) you
are 14.

You are at the party. Walk around the room and greet as many
people as you can.

KEEPING THE CONVERSATION GOING

Warm up: Is he?

Your teacher is going to tell you about a friend. You can show polite interest with falling intonation like this:

Is he?

Did you?

Was it?

You can show real interest or surprise with rising intonation like this:

Is he?

Did you?

Was it?

For example:

T I met Mary yesterday.

S1 Did you?

T Yes, she looks very well.

S2 Does she?

T Yes, she and her husband have just got back from holiday.

S3 Have they?

Before you begin, you can listen to the example on the cassette and repeat the questions.

Recognizing skills

Task 1

You are going to listen to two friends, Gillian and David, talking on the phone. David tells Gillian about his weekend away.
Close your book and listen to the conversation.

Rewind the cassette. Listen again and read silently.

Gillian 341 4754

David Hello. Is that Gillian? David speaking.

Gillian David! How nice to hear you. How are you? Have you had a good weekend?

David Great. I went away actually.

21

Gillian	Oh, did you? Where?
David	Cornwall.
Gillian	How nice.
David	We went to see my grandparents.
Gillian	Really. Where do they live?
David	Near Penzance. In a small village.
Gillian	Ah, right. What was the weather like?
David	Well, pretty awful. It rained all the time.
Gillian	Did it? Oh dear.
David	It didn't matter. We visited friends and did some shopping...
Gillian	Uhum.
David	... and went to Land's End.
Gillian	How interesting.
David	Oh, and we went to a wonderful restaurant. The food was excellent and it was only £12 a head.
Gillian	£12! No. Really?
David	Yes. So, all in all, we had a very good weekend. But what about you? How was your weekend?
Gillian	Well, actually, I spent the weekend in bed.
David	In bed?
Gillian	Yes, I had flu.
David	Did you? I'm sorry to hear that.
Gillian	I'm alright now.
David	Well, look after yourself. Anyway, Gillian ...

Task 2

You are going to hear six exchanges from the conversation. Listen and complete them.

1 I went away actually.   Oh, ... ? .... ?

2 I went to Cornwall.   ....

3 It rained all the time.   ....

4 We went to Land's End. ....

5 Dinner was £12 a head. .... ! No. .... ?

6 I spent the weekend in bed. .... ?

Listen to each exchange again. Mark the second part of each one to show the intonation, like this:

I went away actually.   Oh, did you? Where?

Task 3

You will hear David speaking on the telephone. Play the part of Gillian. Look at the book but don't write her words.

David   I went away for the weekend actually.

Gillian   .... ? .... ?

David   Cornwall.

Gillian   ....

David   We went to see my grandparents.

Gillian   .... live?

David   Near Penzance. In a small village.

Gillian   .... weather .... ?

David   Well, pretty awful. It rained all the time.

Gillian   ....

David   It didn't matter. We visited friends and did some shopping ...

Gillian   ....

David   ... and went to Land's End.

Gillian   ....

David   Oh, and we went to a wonderful restaurant. The food was excellent and it was only £12 a head.

Gillian   .... ! .... ?

David   Yes. So, all in all, we had a very good weekend.

Phrase Box

Encouraging noises and phrases	Uhuh. I see. Yes. Right. OK. Sure. Really? (How) interesting. (How) nice.	
Encouraging by repeating a word	It was an exciting film.	Yes, very exciting.
Questions to keep the conversation going	Where (did you go)? What (did you do next)? Why (did you do it)? How (did you find it)? How often (do you go)? How many (times have you seen it)? Have you ever (seen it)? Do you think (you will go again)?	

Developing skills

Task 1

Work in pairs. Read this conversation by matching the phrases.

A

① – I'm studying Chinese.

– After the programme you can read the grammar and new words.

– On TV.

– Yes, very difficult. But I have a book as well.

– Next year I want to go to Hong Kong. I hope I learn a lot before that.

– I hope so.

B

– Right.

– TV! How interesting! Is it difficult?

– Chinese? Really. Where?

– I'm sure you will.

– Oh, I see.

24

Task 2

Ask your teacher: *What did you do yesterday?* Then encourage your teacher to keep talking by using encouraging noises and phrases and by asking questions. For example:

Interesting.	Where (did you meet him)?
I see.	Who (did you go with)?
Uhuh.	Why (did he buy it)?
Really.	What (did you buy)?
Right.	When (did you get back home?)
	How long (did you wait)?

Using skills

Task 1

Work in pairs. Sit back-to-back, looking in opposite directions. Tell your partner about something, for example:

- what you did at the weekend
- how your bedroom is arranged
- a dream you had last night
- what you are planning to do for the rest of the day
- what you bought last time you went to the supermarket.
- a holiday you have enjoyed

Task 2

Work in pairs. Bring to class an object which you particularly like, a souvenir of your country or a photo. Tell your partner about it. Your partner will use encouraging noises and phrases and ask questions to keep you talking.

EXPLAINING WHAT YOU MEAN

Warm up: What do you call it in English?

Your teacher or a student will think of something. You must ask 'yes/no' questions to find out what it is. For example:

T   I'm thinking of a thingumijig. What do you call it in English?

S1   Is it in the classroom?

T   No.

S2   Can you drink it?

T   Yes.

S3   Do you drink it for breakfast?

T   Yes.

S4   Is it coffee?

Y   Yes.

Recognizing skills

📼 *Task 1*

Mustafa will soon be returning home. He tells his hostess about the souvenirs he has bought for his family. Close your book and listen to the conversation.

Rewind the cassette. Listen again and read silently.

Anne   Did you buy some nice souvenirs, Mustafa?

Mustafa   Yes, but I'm afraid I've packed them.

Anne   Never mind. What did you get?

Mustafa   Well, for my little sister I bought – I'm not sure of the word in English. It's a kind of big cup and it's got a picture on it.

Anne   Ah, you mean a mug. What we use for drinking coffee in the morning.

Mustafa   Yes, that's right. A mug. And for my little brother, oh dear, um, it's made of plastic and it's like snow inside. My little brother collects them. You use it to stop papers blowing away.

Anne   Do you mean a paper-weight?

Mustafa   Yes, a paperweight.

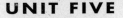

PART ONE

UNIT FIVE

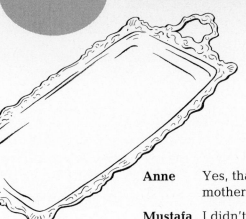

Anne   Yes, that's a nice gift. And what did you get for your mother?

Mustafa   I didn't know what to get her. In the end I got – what do you call it in English? It's a thing for carrying plates and things.

Anne   A tray.

Mustafa   Yes! A tray, made of silver.

Anne   A silver tray! How lovely! And what did you get for your other sister?

Mustafa   A thing that you use for drying dishes. You know what I mean, one with a picture on it.

Anne   A tea cloth?

Mustafa   Yes, that's right. A tea cloth.

Anne   That sounds very nice.

🔲 Task 2

You are going to hear eight phrases from the conversation. Listen and complete them.

1   I'm .... in English.

2   What .... in English?

3   It's .... big cup.

4   It's .... plastic.

5   .... snow.

6   .... stop papers blowing away.

7   .... carrying plates and things.

8   It's .... drying dishes.

🔲 Task 3

You will hear the phrases again with pauses. Listen and repeat, remembering to make links between words.

Phrase Box

Saying you don't know a word	I'm not sure of I don't know	the word (in English). the English for... what it's called in English.
	What do you call it in English?	
Describing	It's like a ... It's made of ...	It's a | sort | of ... | kind |
	It's a thing It's stuff	for (washing dishes) to (wash dishes) you use to (wash dishes)
	It's used You use it	for ... (v + ing) to ... (v)
	It's a |	place where ... thing which/that ... person who ...
Using 'family' words	a mug → a big cup a boat a barge } → a small ship a yacht	
Helping	You mean ...	

Developing skills

Task 1

Work in pairs. **A** and **B** are doing an English vocabulary exercise. Read their conversation by matching the phrases.

A

– What do you call a thing which shows the months of the year?

– A puppy. I don't know the English for a thing you use for cooking.

– Gloves. What's the English for a place where children like to go – where they go and play?

– That's right.

B

– That's easy. A playground. I want the word for a small dog.

– Do you mean a saucepan?

– You mean a calendar. I don't know the English for things you put on your hands when it's cold.

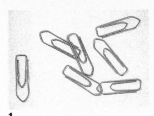

1

Task 2

Work in pairs. Take it in turns to describe one of the people or objects in the pictures, using two or three phrases from the **Phrase Box**. Your partner must guess which number you are describing. For example:

A   I don't know what it's called in English. It's made of wood and you use it to catch mice.

B   Number 10.

2

3

4

5

6

7

8

9

10

11

12

13

14

15

16

When you have finished, you can ask your teacher what the people and objects are called in English.

Using skills

Your teacher will show you some things. You will see each one for only a few seconds. Look but don't write.

When you have seen all the things, write down one sentence for each of the things, using some of these phrases:

It's a kind of ...

It's made of ...

It's like a ...

It's used for ... *or* You use it for ...

Then work in small groups. How many things do you remember? How many different sentences does the group have for each thing?

CLOSING A CONVERSATION

Warm up: Times

Your teacher will ask questions about times and dates. Answer using expressions like these:

at half past six   on January 15th
on Monday   in 1982

Recognizing skills

🔲 *Task 1*

You are going to hear three people leaving a party. Close your book and listen.

Rewind the cassette. Listen again and read silently.

Anne   Eleven o'clock already. Gillian, I really must go.

Gillian   Are you sure?

Anne   Well, I have to get up early tomorrow.

Gillian   Well, it's been lovely to see you. Thanks for coming.

Anne   Thank you. It was a lovely evening. Goodbye.

Gillian   Goodbye.

John   Look, I'm sorry, I really must go or I'll miss the last bus.

Gillian   I quite understand. I'm sorry we can't give you a lift.

John   That's alright. It was good to see you again.

Gillian   Well, keep in touch.

John   Sure. Sorry to rush off like this. But see you. Bye.

Gillian   Bye.

David   Oh! I hadn't noticed the time. I must be off.

Gillian   Are you sure? It's not very late.

David   Well, I have a long day tomorrow. But thank you for a delicious meal.

Gillian   Not at all. See you next week.

David   Yes. I'll be in touch. Goodbye.

Gillian   Bye.

Task 2

You will hear eleven phrases from the conversation. Listen and complete them.

1 Gillian, ... go.

2 I .... off.

3 I'm sorry ....

4 .... get up early tomorrow.

5 .... long day tomorrow.

6 I must go .... miss the last bus.

7 .... lovely evening.

8 .... delicious meal.

9 .... see you again.

10 .... in touch.

11 .... next week.

Task 3

You will hear the phrases again, this time with pauses. Listen and repeat, remembering to make the links between words.

Phrase Box

Pre-closings		
1 Announcing departure	Well... I really must go.	
	(I'm afraid) we should go now.	
	It's getting late.	
	I hadn't noticed the time.	
	Look at the time.	
	Is that the time?	
2 Giving a reason	I have to	get up at ...
		be at X by...
	I have a long day tomorrow.	
3 Thanks and apologies	Thank you for a (lovely evening).	
	It was a (lovely evening).	
	It was good to (see you again).	
	Well, it's been nice talking to you, but I'm afraid ...	
	I'm sorry I have to rush off like this.	
Closings	Goodbye.	
	See you. See you	later.
		tomorrow.
	Come and see me.	
	Keep in touch.	
	I'll be in touch.	
	Give my	best wishes	to ...
		love

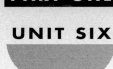
Developing skills

Task 1

Work in pairs. Match the phrases and read the conversations. Take it in turns to be **A** and **B**, **C** and **D**.

A

- I'm sorry, I really must go.

- It was lovely. Goodbye.

- Yes, of course. Thanks for the delicious meal.

- Yes, I have a long day tomorrow.

B

- I'm glad you enjoyed it.

- Well, keep in touch.

- Goodbye. See you.

- Are you sure? It's not very late.

C

- Three o'clock! I hadn't noticed the time. I must go.

- And it was good to see *you*. See you next week.

- Yes. I have to be at the bank by three thirty.

D

- See you.

- Well, it was good to see you.

- Are you sure?

Task 2

Work in pairs. Take it in turns to be **A** and **B**.

B has to leave for a meeting. **A** wants **B** to stay. **B** gives **A** three or four reasons for leaving. For example:

A Must you go?

B Yes, I'm sorry. I have a meeting at ten.

A Can't you stay?

B No, I'm afraid not. I must be on time.

A Must you really go?
Stay a little longer.   etc.

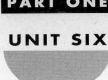

Using skills

Task 1

Work in groups of four or six, divided into pairs. In turn, act out the situation in front of the rest of the group. Then discuss which 'closing' was the most effective and the most polite.

Situation: Two friends, **A** and **B**, have been talking about something that has recently happened (an exam, a party last night, a film they have just seen, etc.) **A** has an appointment and must try to end the conversation politely. **B** wants to go on talking.

Task 2

Work in threes. Take it in turns to be **A**, **B** and **C**.

A and **B** role-play these 'closing' situations. **C** listens and takes notes about the way **A** and **B** close the conversation.
When **A** and **B** finish, **C** discusses the notes with them.

1   *Roles:* two strangers at a bus-stop.

   Scene: You are waiting for a bus. You have started a conversation about the weather when you see **A**'s bus coming. **B** must wait for the next bus. What happens next?

2   *Roles:* two people who have just made friends with each other.

   Scene: You have been talking for about twenty minutes and feel that you have become friends. **B** pauses, then says: 'Well, it was nice talking to you.' What happens next?

3   *Roles:* two friends who know each other well.

   Scene: You have been talking for quite a long time. **A** must leave for an English lesson. What happens next?

4   *Roles:* language school principal, student.

   Scene: You have been discussing a test that the student failed. The principal looks at the clock and says that he/she has a class in fifteen minutes. The student responds.

PART TWO

Conversation Topics

In **Part 2** the conversations are on topics that thousands of people, all over the world, talk about when they meet informally.

Before you start a conversation task give yourself time – at home or in class – to think about the topic.

Use some of the skills that you learned and practised in Part 1.

When you are speaking

1   If you don't know the English for something, try to explain it in different words, or ask the people you are talking with.

2   Help to keep the conversation going by making general statements more specific. For example: *I have a large family. I have three brothers, six cousins, two aunts, a grandmother ...*

3   Have conversations, not monologues, by asking your listeners questions.

4   To be a good speaker you need a big vocabulary. Use the **Vocabulary Boxes** and add your own words to them.

When you are listening

1   Keep the conversation going by asking questions and showing your interest, verbally and non-verbally.

2   Interrupt if you don't understand or if you want the speaker to speak more slowly or clearly.

3   If the speaker doesn't know the English for something, help them if you can.

TALKING ABOUT YOUR FAMILY AND YOURSELF

Warm up: So do I

Your teacher will tell you about herself/himself. Agree with your teacher like this:

T I like classical music.   **S1** So do I.

T I'm not going out tonight.   **S2** Neither am I.

T I am going to stay at home and watch TV.   **S3** So am I.

T I don't like TV quiz programmes.   **S4** Neither do I.

Conversations: Your family

Task 1

Work in pairs. Tell each other about your families. Talk about:

• who is in your family

• their age

• wheré they live

Vocabulary box

great grandparents {	great grandmother great grandfather	
grandparents {	grandmother grandfather	great aunt great uncle
parents { mother stepmother father stepfather	in-laws {	mother-in-law father-in-law

single   wife   aunt
married   husband   uncle
divorced   partner
separated
                                        a teenager
sister   cousin   in his twenties
brother   in her seventies

(adopted) child   daughter   niece
                     son   nephew

grandchildren { granddaughter
                 grandson

Task 2

Work in pairs. Describe a member of your family to your partner.
If possible, show a photo. Talk about his/her:

- physical appearance
- character
- job
- interests   etc.

To keep the conversation going, your partner can ask questions like:

- In what way is she patient?
- When is she bad-tempered?

Vocabulary box

tall/short	fat	plump	slim	thin	
quiet/talkative			patient/impatient		
hardworking/lazy			practical/impractical		
warm/cold			tidy/untidy		
good-tempered/bad-tempered			self-confident/shy		
beautiful	handsome	good-looking			

Conversations: Yourself

Task 1

Work in pairs. Tell each other about a typical day in your life. Then make a group of four with another pair. Introduce your partner to the other two people and tell them about him/her.

Task 2

Work in pairs. Talk about your likes and dislikes. You may want to talk about some of these things:

- cooking • dogs and cats • being alone • reading • pop music
- going to discos • modern architecture • walking in the rain
- travelling by plane • television • small children

Vocabulary box

I love ...	I'm fond of ...	I quite like ...	I dislike ...
I like ...	I'm keen on ...	I don't really like ...	I hate ...

Remember to ask questions to keep the conversation going.

TALKING ABOUT HOMES

Warm up: I don't

Your teacher will tell you about herself/himself. Disagree with your teacher, like this:

T I've got a garden.   **S1** I haven't.

T But I don't like gardening.   **S2** I do.

Conversations: Your home

Task 1

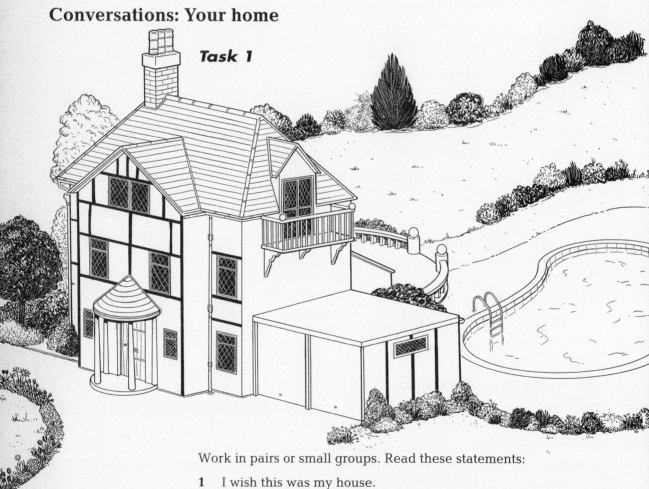

Work in pairs or small groups. Read these statements:

1   I wish this was my house.
2   I'm glad this is not my house.
3   If this was my house, I would change it a little.

Take it in turns to make one of the statements more specific. Use the **Vocabulary Box** on page 41. For example:

I wish this was my house. It's very big and it has a swimming pool, a big garage and a large garden.

Vocabulary box

a (three)-storey house	parking space
a (flat) roof	a garage
the ground floor	a swimming pool
the first floor	a front garden, a back garden
the basement	a garden path
a balcony	a drive
a terrace	a flower bed
a porch	

Now take it in turns to describe the house or flat where you live or your dream house. To keep the conversation going, be sure to make general statements more specific. The others can ask questions, for example:

Where is it exactly?
What can you see from the windows?
How old is it?
Why do you like it?
What changes would you like to make to it?   etc.

Task 2

Make groups of three or four. Make sure there are some people who live in a flat and some who live in a house. Talk about which is best, living in a flat or a house. Think about the good points and the bad points.

Vocabulary box

secure (*n.* security)	comfortable	services
private (*n.* privacy)	noisy	a porter
friendly		a lift
convenient	neighbours	an entryphone

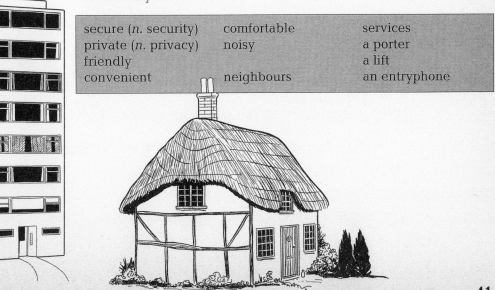

Conversations: Inside the home

Task 1

Draw a plan of your house. Do not label the rooms.

Work in pairs. Explain to your partner what the different rooms are and how you go from one room to another.

Vocabulary box

a kitchen	a staircase the landing
a bathroom	a spiral staircase
(an ensuite bathroom)	a passage
a shower-room	the hallway
a toilet	open plan
a living room	
a dining room	to go up the stairs
a bedroom	to go along the passage
a guest room	
a study	on the | ground | floor
an attic	second
a cellar	

Task 2

Work in small groups. Imagine that each of you is going to have two guests coming to stay: a young friend and an older person. Compare what you will have to do in your home. Think about:

- preparations you will have to make (e.g. put clean sheets on the beds)
- changes to the family routine (e.g. will you have to share the bathroom with your guests?)
- things you tell your guests about (e.g. where the tea and coffee are kept)
- things you warn your guests about (e.g. the cat likes sleeping on the bed)
- house rules (e.g. breakfast is at seven thirty)

TALKING ABOUT EATING

Warm up: Would you like ...? / Do you like ...?

Your teacher will ask you questions.
When the teacher asks *'Would you like (to) ...'*, answer:

Yes, I would. Thank you very much.
Yes, I'd love one. Yes, I'd love to.
That would be lovely.
No, I'm afraid I can't.
No thanks.

When the teacher asks *'Do you like ...'*, answer:

Yes, I do.
Yes, I love it.
Yes, quite.
Not very much.
No, (I'm afraid) I don't.
No, not at all.

Conversations: Eating at home

Task 1

Make a list of food, herbs and spices that you eat and that you know are good for you.

Work in small groups. Talk about why and when you eat the things on your lists.

Vocabulary box

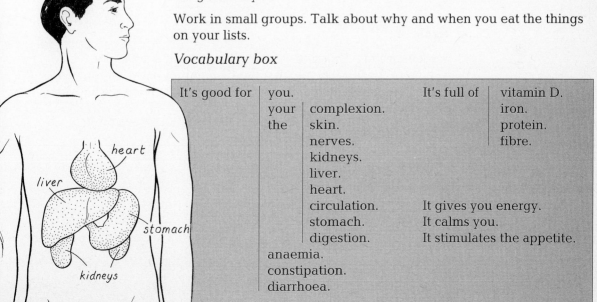

It's good for	you.		It's full of	vitamin D.
	your	complexion.		iron.
	the	skin.		protein.
		nerves.		fibre.
		kidneys.		
		liver.		
		heart.		
		circulation.	It gives you energy.	
		stomach.	It calms you.	
		digestion.	It stimulates the appetite.	
	anaemia.			
	constipation.			
	diarrhoea.			

liver
heart
stomach
kidneys

43

Task 2

Imagine you are going to give a dinner party. You will serve food that is typical of your country. Write out a menu for food and drink.

Do a role play in small groups. One of you is the host or hostess at a dinner party. The others are foreign guests. The food is new to them. Before you start to eat, the host explains what the items are. The guests ask questions, for example to find out what is in the food, how it is prepared, etc.

Repeat the role play with a new host or hostess.

Conversations: Eating in restaurants

Task 1

Work in pairs. Tell each other about a fast food or take-away place you know well. Talk about:

- where it is
- the kind of food it serves
- prices
- opening times
- service
- cleanliness   etc.

Task 2

Work in groups. Imagine you are sitting round a table at a restaurant. Look at the menu opposite and find out what the people in your group can and can't eat and drink. Then decide what you will order.

Vocabulary box

I'm	a vegetarian.	I don't	eat ...
	a Muslim/Hindu.		drink ...
	Jewish.		

I'm allergic to ...

I'm on a diet.

I'm	slimming.		
	trying to	slim.	
		lose weight.	
		put on weight.	

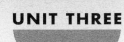
MENU

Starters

Prawn cocktail

Ham with Dijon mustard

Shellfish soup

Avocado cocktail

Mushroom creme surprise

Main courses

Pork spareribs

T-bone steak

Lamb in white wine sauce

King Prawn curry Madras

Grilled fish

Cauliflower with creamy cheese sauce

Onion tart

Spaghetti with mushroom and ham cream sauce

All main courses are served with vegetables, and boiled potatoes, chips or rice.

Desserts

Strawberries and cream

Caramel pudding

Ice cream (chocolate, strawberry, vanilla)

Chocolate gateau

Fresh fruit salad

Cheese-cake

Cheese and biscuits

Drinks

Espresso coffee

Decaffeinated coffee

Tea

Hot chocolate

Milk

Fruit juices (orange, apple)

Wine: please ask for our wine list

TALKING ABOUT CLOTHES AND SHOPPING

Warm up: I hope so

Your teacher will talk to you. Answer using these phrases. Notice that sometimes more than one phrase will be appropriate.

I think so.	I don't think so.
I hope so.	I hope not.
I'm afraid so.	I'm afraid not.

 Before you begin, you can use the cassette to practise saying these phrases. Listen to the phrases. Then listen and repeat.

Conversations: Clothes

Task 1

Work in pairs. Describe to your partner the clothes that you wear on three of these occasions:

- at a party
- at a disco
- at the theatre
- at the weekend relaxing at home
- at an interview

- shopping in town
- at work
- in the countryside
- at a wedding

Which of these clothes do you:

- feel most comfortable in?
- look best in?

Vocabulay box

well	dressed	open-necked	shirt
smartly		short-sleeved	
casually			
cotton (*adj. & n.*)	tie	school uniform	
silk (*adj. & n.*)	belt		
leather (*adj. & n.*)	scarf		
suede (*adj. & n.*)	gloves		
woollen (*adj.*)			
boots	dressing gown	earrings	
slippers	pyjamas	necklace	
trainers	nightdress	brooch	
sandals		bracelet	
high-heeled shoes		ring	

Task 2

What did you wear when you were about five, twelve and sixteen years old? Think about clothes you wore:

- at school
- at weekends
- at night
- on special occasions (e.g. a birthday party)

Bring some photos to class if you can.

Work in small groups. Talk to each other about clothes you used to wear.

Conversations: Shopping

Task 1

Think about what you would spend the following sums of money on:

- £1 • £10 • £50 • £100 • £1000

Work in small groups. Take it in turns to describe what you want to buy with each sum of money. Explain why you want to buy these things.

Task 2

Work in pairs. If you are from the same country, imagine a foreign friend is coming to visit you both for three days. He/she is quite rich. The list shows what he/she wants to buy.

If you are from different countries, take it in turns to imagine you are going to visit your partner's country for three days. You are rich. The list shows what you want to buy.

1   Four souvenirs (two cheap and two expensive ones) to give as gifts.
2   Clothes or jewellery typical of the country.
3   A piece of furniture or other household item typical of the country.

Discuss:

- exactly what to buy.
- which shops to go to.

TALKING ABOUT HOLIDAYS AND FESTIVALS

Warm up: What do you think?

If you can't answer a question, or don't want to, you can try passing it to someone else, like this:

Question: Where is Timbuktu?

Passing it on: What do you think Mary?
I don't know. Alan?
I'm not sure. Do you know, John?
I've no idea. What about you, Peter?
Ask Margaret. She knows.

Your teacher will ask some questions. If you are not sure of the answer, pass the question to another student.

Conversations: Holidays

Task 1

Work in small groups. Look at these statements:

1   When I go on holiday, I always seem to take too much.
2   I don't like travelling by (car/train).
3   I like travelling by (car/train).

Take it in turns to make one of these statements more specific. For example:

I don't like travelling by car. It gets too hot, it's uncomfortable and the motorway is always very busy.

Talk about places you dream of visiting. To help keep the conversation going, be sure to make general statements more specific.

Task 2

Think about a very good holiday you have had. Bring some photos of it if you can. Make notes about it, for example:

* Where did you go?
* Who with?
* For how long?
* Where did you stay?
* Did you meet some interesting people?
* What did you do? see? buy?

- What was the weather like?
- What was the best moment during the holiday?

Work in pairs. Tell each other about the holiday. Remember to encourage each other to talk and ask questions.

Vocabulary box

to go	swimming for a swim	nightlife a beach
to sunbathe to get sunburnt to go sightseeing to hire a car to camp		sports facilities a swimming pool scenery souvenir shops places of interest tourists local people

Conversations: Festivals

Task 1

Think about the main festivals in your country or town. Which two do you think a foreigner would find most interesting?

Work in pairs. **A** is a foreigner. **B** describes and explains one of the festivals. **A** should ask questions to make **B**'s description as specific as possible.

Change roles to describe the second festival.

Task 2

Work in pairs. **A** is a foreigner who has been invited to a wedding in **B**'s town. **A** wants to know:

- what will happen before, during and after the wedding ceremony
- what to wear
- how to behave
- what gift to give

Vocabulary box

bride bridegroom bridesmaid best man		guests wedding dress wedding cake reception
civil religious	ceremony	honeymoon speech

49

TALKING ABOUT WORK AND LEISURE

Warm up: Can and Can't

Your teacher will tell you what Fred and Tom can do. Contradict like this:

T   Fred can swim, can't he?

S1   <u>Fred</u> can't but <u>Tom</u> can.

T   Oh. And Tom can play tennis.

S2   <u>Tom</u> can't but <u>Fred</u> can.

T   And Fred can play football, can't he?

S3   <u>Fred</u> can't but <u>Tom</u> can.

Tom   **Fred**

Before you begin, you can use the cassette to practise pronunciation and stress. Listen to the example. Then listen again and repeat the responses.

Conversations: Work

Task 1

Work in pairs or small groups. Talk to each other about your job or, if you are a student, about your studies. Talk about:

* why and when you decided to study/take the job
* people you meet
* tasks you have to do
* the time you spend working
* the number of days holiday you have
* things you like about it
* things you don't like about it
* how much longer you expect to study/do this job

Use the **Vocabulary Box** on page 51.

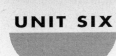

Vocabulary box

regular irregular short long	working hours		to have job satisfaction a (friendly) working atmosphere
a (n)	well-paid badly-paid skilled unskilled stressful creative stimulating boring dangerous	job	a (monthly) salary (weekly) wages perks : a company car travel expenses good promotion prospects

Task 2

Choose one of these jobs to complete the statement:

I'm glad I'm not ...

JOBS
a dentist
a nurse
a policeman
an air hostess
a traffic warden
a piano teacher
a restaurant manager
a farmer
a shop assistant
a housewife
a househusband

Work in small groups. Take it in turns to make your statement more specific. For example:

I'm glad I'm not a housewife. Housewives work very hard, they don't get a salary, etc.

Now talk together about a job that a member of your family does, or your ideal job. Remember to make general statements more specific.

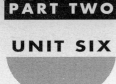

Conversations: Leisure

Task 1

Work in pairs or small groups. Find out what each person's favourite pastime, sport or hobby is.

Ask:
- when they started it
- why they started it
- how much it costs
- where they do it
- what equipment they need
- why they enjoy it

Vocabulary box

> to enjoy (reading)
> to take up (jogging/skiing/chess)
> to take (music) lessons
> to collect (stamps/antiques)
> to join a (tennis club/choir)
> to go to an evening class in (woodwork)

Task 2

Work in pairs. Imagine you arrive at work as usual. Your boss tells you that he/she is giving everyone two days' holiday. Decide how you are going to spend this unexpected free time and write a plan. Include as many things as possible, for example housework (tidy my cupboard) and pleasure (visit my grandmother).

Work in small groups. Show your plan to the others in the group. Explain what you plan to do and your reasons for each decision.

PAIRWORK MATERIAL

A's letter (for Part 1 Unit 2 Task 2, page 15)

```
                                    Edmonton*, Canada.
                                    15 March

Dear A

Thanks for your letter. We all enjoyed your news.
Here is the latest news from us.

Mary has a new peke* so she now has a total of five!
She bought it last week in Saskatoon*.  It has very
pretty markings* but it's very noisy. Everyone thinks
it's going to bite them because it makes so much
noise, so now it has to wear a muzzle*.  The poor dog
is really very friendly and we all love him,.

That's all for today. I hope to hear from you again
soon.
```

Yours
Andrew

* Edmonton: a town in western Canada in the state of Alberta

* a peke: a small dog; a Pekinese, originally from China

* markings: different colours of fur

* a muzzle: to stop it biting

* Saskatoon: a town about 400 kilometres east of Edmonton

B's letter (for Part 1 Unit 2 Task 2, page 15)

Cork*,
Ireland

20 March

Dear B

Thank you for your letter. The family all enjoyed your news. Here is some of ours.

Michael has an old banger*! He bought it for only 65 quid*. It's really beautiful - a black body with green upholstery*, and it has an enormous boot *. He bought it in Galway* and drove it home. We all got such a surprise when we saw him in it.

I can't think of any other news, so I'll stop here. Write soon!

Yours
Louise

* Cork: a town in the south of Ireland.

* a banger = an old car

* upholstery = the covers on the seats of the car

* quid = a pound

* Galway = a town in Ireland, about 140 kilometres from Cork

* boot = at the back of the car, where you put luggage

TEACHER'S NOTES

Teaching Record

The units in Part 1 and Part 2 can be taught in the order that suits your class best. You may wish to move, say, from a unit in Part 1 to a unit in Part 2 and then back to another unit in Part 1.

You can keep a record of what you have taught by putting a tick (3) in the appropriate boxes on the grids.

Part 1	Warm up	Recognizing skills			Phrase Box	Developing Skills		Using Skills	
		Task 1	Task 2	Task 3		Task 1	Task 2	Task 1	Task 2
Unit 1									
Unit 2									
Unit 3									
Unit 4									
Unit 5									
Unit 6									

Part 2	Warm up	Conversations (1)		Conversations (2)	
		Task 1	Task 2	Task 1	Task 2
Unit 1					
Unit 2					
Unit 3					
Unit 4					
Unit 5					
Unit 6					

STARTING A CONVERSATION

Warm up

Before you start the warm up you can use the cassette for 'listen and repeat' practice. These exchanges are on the cassette:

A	OK?	**B**	OK.
A	Ready?	**B**	Ready.
A	Right?	**B**	Right.
A	Finished?	**B**	Finished.
A	Tired?	**B**	Tired.
A	Enough?	**B**	Enough.
A	Yes, I think that's enough.		

Start the warm up like this:

T *We're going to play a kind of game. OK?* (Elicit OK from the students.) *When I ask a question, you can answer with the same words. My voice will go up. Your voice will fall. OK?* (Elicit OK, making sure the students are using a falling intonation.)

Continue like this:

T	*Right?*	**S1**	Right.
T	*Got it?*	**S2**	Got it.
T	*(Paul), are you ready?*	**S3**	Ready.
T	*(John), are you ready?*	**S4**	Ready.
T	*How are you feeling today? Tired/exhausted/fine/OK?*		
T	*How did you come to school? By bus/on foot?*		
T	*What time did you get here? (Nine) o'clock?*		
T	*What's the weather like today? Cold/hot?*		
T	*What's the traffic like this morning? Bad?*		
T	*So, let's stop. Enough?*		

You can ask different students the same question. Once the students understand what they are to do, keep the pace fast and snappy.

The game is of course very artificial. Now that your students have got the idea of answering in this way, encourage them to reply to this kind of question *in context* during the normal flow of classroom activity. You can use questions like:

Ready?   Finished?   Right?
Where did we finish yesterday? Page 16? Task 2?

(Idea from T Woodward, Modern English Teacher 14/2)

Recognizing skills

Task 2

Play each phrase as many times as necessary.

These are the complete phrases:

1 I'd like you to meet Mustafa.
2 My name's Gillian.
3 Where are you from?
4 What about you?
5 Are you here alone or with your family?
6 What do you do?
7 I'm interested in old buildings.
8 Pleased to meet you.

Examples of (a) are:

4 here alone = he ralone; with your = wi thyour
5 what about you = wha tabou tyou
7 I'm interested in old = I mintereste di nold
8 meet you = mee tyou

Examples of (b) are:

1	mee(t) Mustafa	**6**	wha(t) do	**8**	please(d) to

Task 3

Now that the students' attention has been focused on these links, the purpose of this task is to give students an opportunity to say the links. If they have problems with a particular link, give them the model yourself and practise it with them.

Developing skills

Task 1

Encourage the students to look up from their books and look at their partner while they are reading the conversation together. The phrases can be matched to make this conversation:

A Hello. My name's Francis.
B Hello, Francis. Nice to meet you. I'm Jo.
A Where are you from?
B I'm from Canada.
A Where exactly in Canada?
B Montreal. Have you been there?
A No, but I've heard it's a lovely place.
B Yes, it is. How long have you been here?
A About a week. And you?
B About three weeks. I'm here on business.
A I'm here on business too. I'm an engineer. What do you do?
B I work for a bank. Are you with your family?
A No, I'm here alone. And you?
B I'm alone too. I'm single.
A What are you interested in?
B I play golf and I like swimming. What about you?
A I like running – marathon running.
B I prefer walking.

Using skills

Task 1

Ask the students to complete the notes on a small piece of paper or card. During the activity, they can hold it in their hand and glance at it if necessary.

Walk around the room with the students, taking part in the activity. In this way you can monitor particular students and ensure that all students take part.

Task 2

Instead of using the photo in the book, students can bring photos of real friends.

unit 2

MAKING SURE YOU UNDERSTAND

Warm up

Be ready to give the students a true or imaginary account of an event which will elicit questions from them. For the purposes of this exercise, students should pick up on the last item of information in each of your sentences.

You can continue the imaginary account in the example:

I went on holiday last year with my sister.
We went together to New York.
We went there in August.
The journey took twelve hours.
We arrived at ten at night.
We stayed at a small hotel in Manhattan.
It cost about $70 a night.
We stayed six days.
The first day we went up the Empire State Building.
It has 102 floors.
The second day we visited the Metropolitan Art Museum.
The second night we had dinner in a Chinese restaurant.
It was so good that we went there three times.
The third day we did some shopping and I spent about $200.

You can bring the exercise to a close by saying:

I think we'll go on with this exercise for another hour.
(S How long did you say?)
Another hour. But no, perhaps that's enough.

Recognizing skills

Task 2

These are the complete phrases:

1 Sorry, I didn't quite catch that.
2 How do you spell that?
3 I'm sorry. Could you speak more slowly please?
4 I'm sorry, I don't understand. What's 'traffic'?
5 Sorry, could you explain what 'traffic' is?
6 Sorry, could you repeat that please?

Phrase Box

To increase students' exposure to these phrases, use them yourself as often as possible during a lesson. Notice that phrases asking for translation are included. When students don't understand something, you can get them to ask you or another student for a mother-tongue translation.

Developing skills

Task 1

Check that the students know:

* the meaning of *cough*
* how to say 463.014 (four-six-three point zero-one-four)

The phrases can be matched to make this conversation:

A Good morning. Can I help you?
B Yes, I'm looking for a book by Richard Driffield.
A How do you spell 'Driffield'?
B D R I double F I E L D. Richard Driffield.
A And what's the name of the book?
B I'm not sure. But it's about (*cough*) cowboys and Indians.
A Sorry, I didn't quite catch that.
B Cowboys and Indians.
A Ah, I know it. It's called *Cowboys in the Wild West*. Look under DRI 463.014.
B Could you repeat that please?
A Yes. DRI 463.014.
B Thank you very much.

Task 2

Pretend you are going to tell a story. In fact you should never get properly started if the students interrupt you and ask for explanations and spelling. The beginning of your 'story' will go something like this:

You *I'm going to tell you a story about an elf.*
S1 (interrupting) Sorry, could you tell me what an elf is?
You *Yes. An elf is a kind of gnome.*
S2 (interrupting) Excuse me, what is a gnome?
You *A gnome is a kind of pixie.*

Continue in this way explaining that:

A pixie is a kind of goblin.
A goblin is a kind of brownie.
A brownie is a kind of sprite.
A sprite is a kind of fairy.

Finish by saying: *Look, this story is too difficult. Let's try another/something else.*

You can start a second 'story' using this sequence:

I'm going to tell you a story about an old man who lived in a hovel.

Continue (with interruptions from the students):

A hovel is a kind of shack.
A shack is a kind of shed.
A shed is a kind of bothy.
A bothy is a kind of hut.
A hut is a kind of house.

You can finish by saying: *I think this is going to be a boring story. Let's go on to the next task.*

(Idea from JYK Kerr, British Council ELTI, 1975)

Using skills

Give students time to prepare to read their texts aloud. If there is something that neither student in a pair understands, teach:

Let's look it up in the dictionary/ask the teacher.

unit 3

MEETING SOMEONE YOU KNOW

Many of the language phrases in this unit may already be known to the students. The activities allow students to practise using the phrases fluently and quickly, so that they soon become 'second nature', as they are for native speakers.

Warm up

In this warm up it is important to practise the phrases first, as you cannot monitor every student while they walk around the class. Make the students imitate faithfully the intonation of the phrases on the cassette, even if they feel they are exaggerating a little. Walk around the class with the students, taking part in the activity. Remember to clap your hands to indicate the 'change' in the weather.

Recognizing skills

Task 2

These are the complete phrases:

1 Hello John. How are you?
2 Not too bad. How are you?
3 Fine thanks.
4 How's your mother?
5 How are things?
6 I haven't seen you for ages.
7 Have you been sick?
8 I'm sorry to hear that.

Developing skills

Task 1

The phrases can be matched to make this conversation:

A Hi Mary, how are you?
B Fine thanks. And how are you?
A Not too bad.
B I haven't seen you for ages. Are you very busy?
A Quite busy.
B Are you still enjoying the job?
A It's fine. How's your brother?
B Well, he had flu last week.
A I'm sorry to hear that. Is he OK now?
B Yes, pretty good.
A There's Alan. I must say hello.
B OK. I'll speak to you later.

Using skills

Notice that taking on the role of a person of a very different age from themselves can help students to relax. This is a technique that you can of course use in many other pair and group activities.

unit 4

KEEPING THE CONVERSATION GOING

Warm up

Point out to the students the difference in meaning created by using falling and rising intonation in the question forms. Falling intonation shows polite interest. Rising intonation is used to show real interest and surprise.

Tell the students about an imaginary or a real friend, pausing after each sentence to give them time to show their interest. Your sentences should include a variety of tenses and persons. You could continue the example like this:

I met Mary yesterday.
She looks very well.
She and her husband have just got back from holiday.
They had a very unusual holiday.
They sailed across the Atlantic.
They've only got a small boat.
It took them ten days.
They were lucky.
The weather was marvellous.

I would love to do something like that.
But I always get seasick.
Mary has always loved boats.
Next year Mary and her husband are planning to sail round the world.
But I think they'll buy a bigger boat.
It will cost a lot.
But Mary's aunt died last year and left her a lot of money.
So they'll use that money to buy the boat.
It'll take them about a year, I think.

Well, that's the end of this exercise.

Recognizing skills

Task 2

Here are the responses in the exchanges, with the intonation marked.

1 Oh, did you? Where?
2 How nice.
3 Oh dear.
4 How interesting.
5 £12. No. Really?
6 In bed?

Developing skills

Task 1

The phrases can be matched to make this conversation:

A I'm studying Chinese.
B Chinese? Really. Where?
A On TV.
B TV! How interesting. Is it difficult?
A Yes, very difficult. But I have a book as well.
B Right. (*or:* Oh, I see.)
A After the programme you can read the grammar and new words.
B Oh, I see. (*or:* Right.)
A Next year I want to go to Hong Kong. I hope I learn a lot before that.
B I'm sure you will.
A I hope so.

Task 2

Either give a true account or invent an account of something you did recently with a friend, For example:

Yesterday I went shopping with (the Prime Minister). The students' questions will to some extent determine the direction the account takes.

Using skills

Task 1

Sitting back-to-back gives students practice in talking in a situation where feedback is only verbal. This is like talking on the telephone.
Students will have to talk louder to their partners than they usually do in pair work. If it is not possible to have all students doing the activity simultaneously because of the noise level, get the students to work in fours. The two students not taking part in the conversation should monitor it and then give language feedback.

Task 2

If your class is of mixed nationalities, or you are of a different nationality from the students, you can ask them to bring some souvenir typical of their country and explain how it is made, when it is used, etc.

unit

EXPLAINING WHAT YOU MEAN

Warm up

The aim of this warm up is to give students practice in asking lots of quick, short questions. If the pace becomes slow, give a few hints, using some of the phrases from the phrase box.

Recognizing skills

Task 2

Here are the complete phrases:

1 I'm not sure of the word in English.
2 What do you call it in English?
3 It's a kind of big cup.
4 It's made of plastic.
5 It's like snow.
6 You use it to stop papers blowing away.
7 It's a thing for carrying plates and things.
8 It's a thing that you use for drying dishes.

Developing skills

Task 1

The phrases can be matched to make this conversation:

A What do you call a thing which shows the months of the year?
B You mean a calendar. I don't know the English for things you put on your hands when it's cold.
A Gloves. What's the English for a place where children like to go – where they go and play?
B That's easy. A playground. I want the word for a small dog.
A A puppy. I don't know the English for a thing you use for cooking.
B Do you mean a saucepan?
A That's right.

Task 2

The people and objects are:

1   Paperclips   2   Scales

3	A hole puncher	10	A mousetrap
4	A model	11	A lifeguard
5	A vase	12	A TV producer
6	A judge	13	A stapler
7	A pilot	14	A vicar (priest)
8	A lipstick	15	Head phones
9	A tin opener	16	A personal organiser

Using skills

This is a variation on Kim's Game. Have ready about fifteen to twenty different items. It is best to use items that students don't know the English words for, and items that are made of a variety of materials, for example: a drawing pin, glue, a plug, tweezers, a mirror, a magnifying glass, a shell, a napkin, a handkerchief, a toothpick, a pepper grinder, a match, a coin, etc.

When the students ask what the people and objects are called, remind them of the phrases they learned in Unit 2. Encourage them to ask about spelling.

Ask students to put down their pens and not write anything. Take the items out from a bag one at a time and hold each one up for a second or two before hiding it again. (Alternatively you can display all the items together for about a minute, as in the picture on page 30.)

When you have finished showing the items, ask the students to write their sentences silently. Give them a few minutes to do this before they move into groups. If you have a small class, you can chack with the whole group which items they remember. Ask a student to give you a sentence, take the appropriate item out of the bag and ask for other sentences about it. Continue in the same way for all the items they remember.

unit 6

CLOSING A CONVERSATION

Warm up

Ask the students questions about:

- their birthdays
- events in childhood
- important historical events
- school or college events
- timetables   etc.

Recognizing skills

Task 2

These are the complete phrases:

1 Gillian, I really must go.
2 I must be off.
3 I'm sorry to rush off.
4 I have to get up early tomorrow.
5 I have a long day tomorrow.
6 I must go or I'll miss the last bus.
7 Thank you. It was a lovely evening.
8 Thank you for a delicious meal.
9 It was good to see you again.
10 I'll be in touch.
11 See you next week.

Developing skills

Task 1

The phrases can be matched to make these conversations:

A I'm sorry, I really must go.
B Are you sure? It's not very late.
A Yes, I have a long day tomorrow,.
B Well, keep in touch.
A Yes, of course. Thanks for the delicious meal.
B I'm glad you enjoyed it.
A It was lovely. Goodbye.
B Goodbye. See you.

C Three o'clock! I hadn't noticed the time. I must go.
D Are you sure?
C Yes. I have to be at the bank by three thirty.
D Well, it was good to see you.
C And it was good to see you. See you next week.
D See you.

Using skills

Tasks 1 and 2

If necessary, students can hold their book and look at the **Phrase Box** while they act. The role-play situations are suggested in 'Developing pragmatic awareness : closing the conversation' by K Bardovi-Harlig et al, ELTJ, Vol. 45/1.

unit 1

TALKING ABOUT YOUR FAMILY AND YOURSELF

Warm up

You can make true or imaginary statements about yourself like these. Try to make both positive and negative statements and use a variety of tenses. Depending on the level of your class, you may also decide to include some statements with modals (may, might, should, etc.)

I often go to concerts.
I don't like pop music.
I don't like jazz.
But I like classical music.
I'm going to a concert tomorrow - a concert of classical music.
I'm going with a friend.
I've already bought tickets.
I bought them about a month ago.
Well, perhaps I'll see you at the concert ...

But tonight I'm not going out.
I'm going to stay at home.

I'll just sit and watch TV.
I don't know what I'll watch.
Not 'Top of the Pops'. I never watch that.
Not a quiz programme. I don't like quiz programmes.
And I won't watch the soap opera.
But I'll watch the news.
And I hope there's a good film on.
And then I'll probably go to bed early.
I'm tired.
I need a good night's sleep.

Well, I think we should stop this exercise and do something different.

Conversations: Your family

Tasks 1 and 2

Ask the students to bring a photo of some members of their family for this activity.

unit 2

TALKING ABOUT HOMES

Warm up

You can make true or imaginary statements about yourself like these. Try to make both positive and negative statements and use a variety of tenses.

I've got a garden.
But I don't like gardening.
It's very hard work.
I wish I lived in a flat.
Well, why don't you come and do some gardening for me?

I've got a swimming pool.
I can't swim.
I didn't learn at school.
I'm frightened of water.
And I think it's too cold to swim.
I haven't got a swimming costume.
Well, come and use my pool.

I've got a garage.
I've got a car.
I'm a good driver.
I learned to drive when I was eighteen.
And I can drive out into the country whenever I want.
I love walking in the country.

I'll go for a long walk in the country next Sunday.
Come with me. You'll enjoy it.
You will.
I won't walk very far.
And I won't walk very fast.
You won't get tired.
You'll get bored staying at home.

You're bored doing this exercise, I'm sure...

Conversations: Your home

Task 1

If the students query the use of 'was' instead of 'were' in 'I wish this was my house', tell them that both can be used. However 'was' is used very frequently in colloquial English.

Conversations: Inside the home

Task 1

Students can draw the plan at home before the lesson. As well as describing the layout of their home, the students can describe features of the interior decoration, the furniture, where their pet dog sleeps, etc.

unit 3

TALKING ABOUT EATING

Warm up

Try to mix up the two types of question and include a few changes of pronoun. This ensures that students listen to the question and do not give mechanical answers.

If a student gives a negative answer that stops your sequence of questions, pass the question to another student.

You can use questions like these:

Would you like to go out this evening?
Do you like going to restaurants?
Do you like hot Indian food?
Do you like Chinese food?
Does your friend like Chinese food?
Would you both like to go out to a Chinese restaurant with me?

Do you like swimming?
Would you like to go swimming tomorrow?
Would you like to bring a friend?
Do you like getting up early?
Would you like to go swimming before work?

Do you like listening to jazz?
Would you like to go to a jazz concert on Monday?
Would your friends like to come too?
Do they like jazz?

Do you like trying to speak English?
Do you like meeting people?
Would you like to meet some American friends of mine?
Would you like to come round this evening?
Would you like to bring some friends?
Do they like pizza?
Would you all like to come and join us for a pizza?

You can finish the exercise by asking: *Would you like to do something different now?*

Conversations: Eating at home

Task 1

If necessary, explain that herbs are the leaves, stems and flowers of plants and are usually used fresh. Spices are the dried parts of aromatic plants, usually from the tropics.

To get the students talking, you can encourage them to think of specific situations, for example when they have overeaten, got sunburnt, stayed up all night working, felt nervous before an exam, etc.

Ask students to prepare the list of food, herbs and spices at home. They can use a dictionary to find the English for items they don't know.

Task 2

Ask students to write the menu as homework before the lesson. This is important as there will probably be quite a lot of new vocabulary that they will need to look up.

Lay a table for each group with some plates and appropriate cutlery. For example, if you have a Chinese or Japanese student he/she can explain to the 'guests' how to use chopsticks.

If your students are all of the same nationality, you may have to encourage them to play their roles as foreign guests who know nothing about the food their host has prepared. If necessary, remind them to use phrases from Part 1 Unit 2, for example *How do you spell that? What is a (cucumber)? Could you explain what a (cucumber) is?*

Although it is of course artificial for students of the same nationality to explain aspects of their shared culture to each other, this type of task is an important rehearsal for communication with people of other nationalities. See also Unit 5 Conversations: Festivals Tasks 1 and 2.

Conversations: Eating in Restaurants

Task 2

If your students do not know any fast food or take-away places, ask them to talk about a café, a street food stall, a bar, a pub, a canteen or a restaurant that they know well.

unit 4

TALKING ABOUT CLOTHES AND SHOPPING

Warm up

Check that the students understand what *a (shopping) sale* and *bargains* mean. You can then ask questions and make statements like these:

There's a sale on at (X) department store. Are you going to go?
It may be very crowded.
But there will probably be lots of bargains.
Some of the items will be very cheap.
But you'll have to get there early.
Are you going to buy any clothes in the sale?
I'm thinking of buying a leather coat. They're expensive, aren't they?
Do you think it'll be a lot cheaper in the sale?
And will you buy some jewellery?
A necklace? Some earrings?
And what about some furniture?
I'd like a new computer. Is it good to buy one in a sale?
A good computer is expensive, isn't it?
Well, I may spend a lot of money at the sale.
I may spend an enormous amount of money!
But I hope I won't.

Conversations: Clothes

Task 1

In the Vocabulary Box point out that *cotton, silk, leather* and *suede* can be used either as adjectives or nouns, for example: *a leather jacket; a jacket made of leather.*

Task 2

If your students are teenagers, you can choose different ages, for example five, nine and twelve.
Encourage students to bring some old photos to class.

Conversations: Shopping

Task 1

If necessary, be ready to tell the students how much £1 is in their own currency. Then ask them to calculate, in English, how much the other sums are.

unit 5

TALKING ABOUT HOLIDAYS AND FESTIVALS

Warm up

You can ask questions like these:

I'm going to Australia for my holidays. What is the capital of Australia? (Canberra)
What is Sydney famous for? (opera house; harbour bridge)
Are there camels in Australia? (yes)
Why do camels have humps? (The hump is a store of fat.)
Why do kangaroos have pockets in the front? (to keep their young safe)
What is a wallaby? (a kind of kangaroo)
What are Aborigines? (the indigenous people of Australia)
What is a kookaburra? (a bird)
What is a didgeridoo? (an Aboriginal musical instrument)

Conversations: Festivals

Tasks 1 and 2

If you have a multi-national class, they may find it more interesting to work in small groups instead of pairs.

If your students are all of the same nationality, you may have to encourage the 'A' students to play their roles as foreigners who know nothing about the festivals or wedding customs of the country. If necessary, remind them to use phrases from Part 1 Unit 2, for example *How do you spell that? What is a ... ? Could you explain what a ... is?*

Although it is of course artificial for students of the same nationality to explain aspects of their shared culture to each other, this type of task is an important rehearsal for communication with people of other nationalities. See also Unit 3 Conversations: Eating at Home Task 1.

TALKING ABOUT WORK AND LEISURE

Warm up

Unlike American English, British English makes a clear distinction in the strong form of the vowel in can /kæn/ and can't /ka:nt/. Students who don't make this vowel distinction are often misunderstood.

You can talk about Tom and Fred like this:

Fred can swim, can't he?
Oh. And Tom can play tennis.
And football? I think Fred can play it, can't he?
And Tom can play rugby, can't he?
And Fred can play cricket.
Well, Fred can play golf.
Are you sure? Fred can play squash, can't he?
Really? So I suppose Tom can play basketball and Fred can't.

Well, I seem to be wrong all the time. I must have got their names wrong. Fred must be Tom and Tom must be Fred ...

You could repeat the exercise using musical instruments. For example:

Fred can play the violin, can't he?